TIED DOWN IN THE SPIRIT

Dr. D. K. Olukoya

TIED DOWN IN THE SPIRIT

ISBN: 978 - 38233 - 3 - 7
1st Printing – June 2005 AD

Published by:
The Battle Cry Christian Ministries
11, Gbeto Street, Off Iyana Church Bus Stop, Iwaya Road, Iwaya, Yaba, P.O. Box 12272, Ikeja, Lagos.
Website: www.battlecrying.com
Email: batlecrying@representattive.com
Phone: 0803-304-4239, 0803-332-2376, 0803-306-0073, 0802-303-3938, 0803-309-8246, 0803-315-7249, 0803-305-4142.

FOREIGN CORRESPONDENCES
UNITED STATES
Phone: 404 – 454 – 3358

GHANA
Phone: 24236113

All scripture quotations are from the King James version of the Bible.
Cover illustration: Sis Shade Olukoya

TABLE OF CONTENT

CHAPTER ONE

TIED DOWN IN THE SPIRIT

When God spoke in the book of Genesis order, came out of disorder. By the time he spoke on, the satanic revival was quenched. I believe the Lord is about to speak once again to you. This message will speak revival to your soul if you are dead spiritually. The confused will receive order and faith in their heart. Are you relegated to the background by dark forces? You will obtain great deliverance.

The book of 1 John has this to say;

1 John 5:19: And we know that we are of God, and the whole world lieth in wickedness.

The whole world lies in wickedness. This implies that man dwells in wickedness and carries out his activities in an environment characterized by wickedness.

CLASSIC EXAMPLES OF WICKEDNESS

Let us consider a kind of terrible wickedness in the Bible

Zech. 5:5-8: Then the angel that talked with me went forth, and said unto me, Lift up now thine eyes, and see what is this that goeth forth. And I said, What is it? And he said, This is an ephah that goeth forth. He said moreover, This is their resemblance through all the earth. And, behold, there was lifted up a talent of lead: and this is a woman that sitteth in the midst of the ephah. And he said, This is wickedness. And he cast it into the midst of the ephah; and he cast the weight of lead upon the mouth thereof.

The interpretation of the wickedness described here shows that it is possible for the spirit of man to be captured and put into bondage. That was what happened to the woman described in the above reference.

A pregnant woman was brought for prayers, many years ago. Her condition was very strange. Whenever she was pregnant, food would be odious and distasteful to her.

She would be feeling as if she should be eating grass, chalk, ashes, water and palm oil. Any time she was pregnant, those were her food. Her husband was therefore following her about in order to force her to eat normal food. She was dragged to someone who claimed to be a deliverance minister. The deliverance minister kept her in a room for three days. At the end of the three days in the house, the deliverance minister raped her! She was then taken away from the so-called deliverance minister.

When she came to see us the Lord revealed that the woman was no longer in her body as she was tied down somewhere in the spirit and fed with grass. The manifestation of what happened in the spirit realm was what was happening to her in real life. Can you see the wickedness of the people of the world?

Whatever cages a person and does not allow him/her to move freely is wickedness.,

There are many who are fighting what they do not know. They found out that all the efforts they make towards moving forward in life proved abortive. It was like someone who came from the race of the Amorites.

Genesis 15:16: But in the fourth generation they shall come hither again: for the iniquity of the Amorites is not yet full.

A curse tied down the Amorites to the same spot. They kept on starting afresh regardless of the position they have attained. No matter how rich the children of the Amorites may be they will relapse into poverty. No matter how far they go, something will still return them back to the lower rung of the ladder.

Something mysterious had fixed them to one spot.

A particular boy excelled in the primary school and then went to the secondary school. During his first year in the secondary school, his grandmother came to visit them. A strange thing then happened one night. The mother of the boy woke up in the middle of the night and something instructed her, "Go to grandma's room". When she got there, she was amazed and troubled by what she saw. She saw her grown up child being breast-fed by the grand mother right from the day the boy was breast fed by the grandmother, there was no progress for the boy. The boy almost became an imbecile, a redundant being until the Lord delivered him in one of our meetings when he began to vomit white substance as a result of the milk which he drank from the grandmother's breast. The incident was a little bit easier to handle because the source of the boy's problem was known. What of those who do not know the source of their problem?

A lot of wicked things are generally done in order to injure the spirit of man. The Bible says that the spirit of man is the candle of the Lord. It searches the inner most parts of the body. The enemy knows that the spirit of man is the candle of Lord and that is why he often makes efforts towards dealing with the candle of the Lord.

The devil generally sponsors lots of wicked actions against the spirit of man. A person may look normal but his spirit man could be under bondage. It is the flesh that pretends; the spirit man does not pretend.

The spirit of man is the candle of the Lord and if that candle is quenched, the person will fail forever.

The wicked has devised evil plans against the spirit of man.

The unfortunate thing is that God's people have continued to perish as a result of lack of knowledge.

THE HAVOCS THAT COULD BE DONE AGAINST THE SPIRIT MAN

The following things could be done against the spirit of man

1. The spirit of man can be arrested.
2. The spirit can be caged.
3. The spirit man can be oppressed.
4. The spirit of a man can be possessed.

This occurs when the spirit of man is captured by an evil spirit. Immediately this happens, another spirit will begin to talk through the person while his or her own spirit is silenced. It is not possible for a spirit-filled believer to be possessed. But if he or she backslides anything can happen.

5. The spirit man can be harassed.

6. The spirit man can be tormented.

7. The spirit man can be weakened in such a way that he cannot pray and read the Bible. If he reads the Bible he will forget. Such people will be pursued by evil.

8. The spirit man can be transferred. It is possible to take the spirit of a person out of him and replace it with a strange spirit. The person then assumes a new personality. When angels of God are dispatched to give the person certain packages, he would miss the blessings because he is not in his position having assumed another personality.

9. The spirit man can be buried.
10. The spirit man can be abused.
11. The spirit man can be perverted.
12. The spirit man can be infested with spiritual disease.

13. The spirit man can be amputated. For example, the Bible teaches that if join yourself with a strange woman, then you and the woman have become one flesh. By the time you sleep with several women, then you have fragmented your spirit man into various departments. It will take the spirit of God to gather the fragmented spirits together and make it wholesome again. That is why God frowns at the sins of sexual immorality. Of all the sins in the Bible, God Himself supervises the repercussions of the sin of fornication.

14. The spirit man can be burdened. That is, the spirit man can be pressed down.

15. The spirit can be rendered insane. It is not only those who are found in psychiatrist hospitals who are mad. There are many mad people with beautiful clothes walking around the streets.

There is a type of manifestation of decent madness in people's lives. The person may be going quietly on the streets clothed with expensive dresses but internally, he is crazy. He has been rendered insane by wicked spirits. Imagine a man who got his wife and daughter pregnant and the strange fellow conducted the naming ceremony of his daughter's child and that of his wife the same day. Is this not madness?

A man has two wives. He could not feed the wives neither could he feed himself and yet begins to plan on marrying a third wife. Such a man is simply out of his mind.

16. The spirit man can be paralysed. In this case all the parts of the body are complete but he cannot move them.
17. The spirit man can be enslaved. Satan is a wicked taskmaster. He will always push men to commit sin and do things contrary to their wish.

I wept the day I saw drug addicts who littered the parks in Lagos. They came begging me for money. I was surprised at the little boys. But when I took a closer look, I saw tiny holes on them. They simply needed money to buy more drugs to inject themselves with.

The demons of drug addiction invaded Nigeria in the form of marijuana or Indian hemp and it was those whose matter had been concluded by household wickedness that engaged in smoking such harmful weeds. But foreign drugs such as cocaine and heroine are now here with us. They enslave men and women alike.

Women are not used to getting drunk in this country before. Now, we have a lot of women drunkards around us. They drink themselves to stupor. What happened to these unfortunate people was that their spirit man had been enslaved.

18. The spirit man can be demoted.
19. The spirit man can be polluted.
20. The spirit man can be rendered blind, deaf and dumb.
21. The spirit man can be made to go into slumber.
22. The spirit man can be bewitched. It will keep repeating the same errors.

23. The spirit man can be remotely controlled.

24. The spirit man can be initiated into evil either consciously or unconsciously.

25. The spirit man can be married off and the person will not know that an evil marriage had taken place.

26. The spirit man can be broken. That is why the Bible talks about broken spirit.

27. The spirit man can be tied down to one spot.

LIMITED AND RESTRICTED

The evil spirit ties down the spirit man to make him suffer limitations in life. There is a spirit called the spirit of limitation. There are some powers called limiting powers. The victim of these powers continues to be limited in all spheres of life until the spirit is dealt with and conquered. There will be limitation physically, spiritually, academically, maritally, financially.

To suffer limitation in life is to have one's level of joy and achievement determined by the enemy. That is, a barrier is created and placed on the life of the person. All the potentials for greatness, excellence and prosperity may be there but there will be an extent to which they are allowed to function if the curse of limitation is in pace.

There is a spiritual rope around the neck of the victim. This rope limits him and so progress in life is determined by the enemy. It is very unfortunate that many people languish in complete darkness concerning the plans of the enemy for their life. Let us look at an important passage in this regard.

Mark 11:1-9: And when they came nigh to Jerusalem, unto Bethphage and Bethany, at the mount of Olives, he sendeth forth two of his disciples, And saith unto them, Go your way into the village over against you: and as soon as ye be entered into it, ye shall find a colt tied, whereon never man sat; loose him, and bring him. And if any man say unto you, Why do ye this? say ye that the Lord hath need of him; and straightway he will send him hither. And they went their way, and found the colt tied by the door without in a place where two ways met; and they loose him. And certain of them that stood there said unto them, What do ye, loosing the colt? And they said unto them even as Jesus had commanded: and they let them go. And they brought the colt to Jesus, and cast their garments on him; and he sat upon him. And many spread their garments in the way: and others cut down branches off the trees, and strawed them in the way. And they that went before, and they that followed, cried, saying, Hosanna; Blessed is he that cometh in the name of the Lord.

The lives of many people can be likened to the conduct of the donkey mentioned in this passage. They are tied down by their household wickedness and witchcraft.

A donkey has potentials but it cannot be used as long as it remains tied.

If a goat is tied by a ten meter rope the goat's sphere of operation is only 10 meters. The testimony of breakthroughs which people give might not be the highest level of blessings which God has designed for their lives. When something is tied down it will remain limited. But there is something better. After a tied goat has finished eating everything within the reach of the ten-meter radius, it will not be able to move forward, although there may be better grasses somewhere else. Its freedom will be restricted to the ten meters allowed by the rope of wickedness.

Sometimes ago, a professor in Nigeria was jailed because he embezzled money that was supposed to be used to procure rice for the benefit of the villagers. When he was dragged to the prison he made an utterance saying, "I belong to the wasted generation". If you do not want to be wasted, you must cry unto God so that he will set you free and use you. This same rope needs to be broken in our national and environmental lives. Many of the best Nigeria professors are no longer here, they are in Saudi Arabia, Kuwait and places like China trying to make money. It will be difficult to blame them for leaving the country for greener pastures when during the time they were in the country, many of them could hardly afford to ride a good car. But when they got to foreign countries they were given better cars and provided with better living conditions. They prefer to stay in their country but the harsh economic condition has discouraged them. This is a kind of bondage.

Judges 6: 25-26: And it came to pass the same night, that the LORD said unto him, Take thy father's young bullock, even the second bullock of seven years old, and throw down the altar of Baal that thy father hath, and cut down the grove that is by it: And build an altar unto the LORD thy God upon the top of this rock, in the ordered place, and take the second bullock, and offer a burnt sacrifice with the wood of the grove which thou shalt cut down.

There is a better ground than where you are at the moment. It is a more prosperous field ahead. Break the yoke that ties you down and watch the power of God catapult your destiny to uncommon heights.

God wanted to use Gideon but certain things in his father's house would not allow God to use him. God could not use Gideon until he threw down the altar of Baal and replaced it with the altar of God. The potentials of Gideon were not realized until he dealt with the altar of his father's house.

Many lives have been destroyed right from the womb. Such lives end up living with limitations.

A limited man is a restricted man. A restricted man may remain in the midst of opportunities and possibilities but can not take advantage of them. Many were told by the enemy, "You will see it but will not taste of it".

Take up this prayer point now with all the available strength you could gather.

Every power saying, "I will see but not taste out of it" die in the name of Jesus".

When a person is limited, he makes tremendous efforts and expects great achievement but nothing is achieved.

To be tied down is to be allowed to operate within a spot. To be tied down in the spirit is to make a person befriend expired people. It is to make a person addicted to dead churches. To be tied down is to make someone get married to a deficit. It means to make a person or group of persons subjected to collective captivity, such as the captivity of poverty. To be tied in the spirit means to put a person in a wrong business or career. To be tied down in the spirit is to introduce a mark of hatred on a person. Wherever he goes, people will not want him around. If you have such a problem, you will notice that those who wanted you around before may no longer want you around. To be tied down is to suffer from lack of helpers, hence, there is no one to offer help. To be tied down is for the enemy to introduce profitless hard work into your life.

To be tied down in the spirit is to suffer prolonged abuse. It is to remain permanently unemployed. It is to suffer redundancy.

There is no height you can reach from where you cannot fall from as long as the rope remain on your neck. The spirit of Kadesh Barnea may still catch up with you if the rope remains attached to your neck.

THE WAY OUT

1. Repent from every known sin, so that the evil rope can be broken. Sin is a heartache to God. God is always against sin because sin has always destroyed what God loves most. What does God loves most? It is you. Sin is a destroyer. The grace that enabled you to say "Yes" to Jesus when you were born again, can enable you to say "No" to sin. Sin brings fear and confusion. Sin is a serious matter with God. Stop sinning before sin stops you. Sack iniquity before it sacks you. There are things you must stop now. If you refuse to stop them now, you may not have the opportunity to stop them again and regrets may follow. Every sin you fail to deal with has power to deal with you.

If Samson had repented a day before his calamity, he would not have experienced the troubles which he went through. Sin has many heads you cannot deal with at once. You must cut it off one after the other. Any sin in your life that allows the enemy to tie you down to one sport must be dealt with.

We were praying for a person whose spirit was tied down many years ago. The problem he had was that he would pluck his hairs and began to eat it. Sometimes he would scratch his skin until he was bleeding. He was tied down in the spirit. But thank God who delivered the man from the bondage of the enemy.

2. The spirit is very complicated. To be free you must pray hard.

A CASE STUDY

Many years ago, there was a bright and intelligent medical doctor she graduated as a specialist doctor and she specialized in the most modern aspect of medicine. She opened a wonderful clinic somewhere with several state-of-the-art medical equipment imported from overseas. The unfortunate thing was that no body was patronizing her. She came to us for prayer. As prayer was going on the Lord showed us three small trees. The Lord said, "She is inside one of the trees. We were worried and asked the Lord, "How can she be inside a tree". The Lord said, we should ask her a question pertaining to the number of children her parents had. She said, "three".

We then asked her again, "When you were born did your parents plant a tree for you?" She said, "yes". She then expatiated further. In the family when a child is born, the placenta would be buried and a tree would be planted on top of the placenta. She said, further, that the tree was still growing in their compound. We told her, "Madam we must deal with that tree" She said, "there is no way you will deal with the tree without my father knowing". We planned a spiritual coup that day. The woman drove to the village and packed her car afar off. She then called somebody and told him to go and uproot a particular tree from her father's compound. She agreed to pay the person. The job was done while she stood afar off watching and waiting for the job to be completed. The hired man completed the job and dragged the tree towards her car.

Immediately the tree was uprooted the father screamed where he was. He ran out but it was too late. That was how the medical doctor was able to move forward in life.

PRAYER POINTS

1. **Every conspiracy against me in the heavenlies, places, be scattered in the name of Jesus.**
2. **Oh thou that troubleth my Israel, the God of Elijah shall trouble** you today in the name of Jesus.
3. **Oh God arise! And make me your battle axe today in Jesus name.**
4. **Powers of limitation, power of unprofitable detentions be die in the name of Jesus.**
5. **Every rope of darkness tying me down to one spot be destoryed in the name of Jesus.**

6. Every ancient gate shut against my life and progress open by fire in the name of Jesus.

7. Every power of my father's house speaking failure into my progress die in the name of Jesus.

8. Let the anointing upon my head, speak against failure in the name of Jesus.

9. I bring the caterpillar of the Lord against every limitation working against my life in the name of Jesus.

10. Every power of bewitchment upon my spirit man die in the name of Jesus.

CHAPTER TWO

THE PROBLEMS OF CLOSED DOORS

"Every conspiracy against my destiny in the heavenlies scatter in the name of Jesus".

"Every organized wickedness fashioned against my breakthrough scatter in the name of Jesus".

CLOSED DOORS

Let us read about one of the popular parables in the Scripture

Matthew 25:8-10: And the foolish said unto the wise, Give us of your oil; for our lamps are gone out. But the wise answered, saying, Not so; lest there be not enough for us and you: but go ye rather to them that sell, and buy for yourselves. And while they went to buy, the bridegroom came; and they that were ready went in with him to the marriage: and the door was shut.

What happens when a person wants to enter into a particular place and all of a sudden the door gets shut? The moment the door is shut admittance is ruled out.

Doors are very interesting entities. They are amazing inventions. Doors can either let you in or shut you out. You cannot call something a door except it can move back and forth. Most of the time locks and keys are used for the doors.

LOCKED OUT

When a person is locked out, there are several things that happen outside the door. One major thing that would happen is frustration or disappointment. This will lead to distress and anger. The person who is locked outside the door will be exposed to hard conditions. The bottom line is that once a person can not gain access to where he or she is going because the door is shut ,frustrations and all kinds of internal and external hardship would set in.

The power of closed doors should not be taken lightly. It should not be handled with levity. I felt sorry for a minister I once counseled. He started a particular church and made his first tragic mistake. He appointed a powerful committee as elders. Eventually the committee became a giant committee. The members of the committee started to control the pastor. He then told them, "I am the one that chose you, therefore you cannot start to control me".

One day, he called the meeting of the council of elders. He said to them, "Since you people are bent on controlling me, I dissolve you in the name of the Father, Son and the Holy Spirit. This committee is hereby dissolved". To the amazement of the pastor, the committee members faced him and said, "We refuse to be dissolved in Jesus name. In the name of the father, the son and the Holy Spirit we revoke your statement". Confusion set in and there was an open fight. That was the end of his first attempt in establishing a ministry.

In his second attempt, the church had been established and had started to grow. There was a baptismal ceremony that was to take place at the river side. A pregnant woman was one of those that came to be baptized. The woman drowned! She died! Again, that was the end of the second ministry.

He tried one more time. The third attempt was more horrible. As the church progressed, the pastor developed interest in his driver's wife and started to commit adultery with her. He made her pregnant. That was the end of the third attempt in ministry.

What happened to the pastor was that the door of ministry was closed to him. There is no amount of struggling and activities outside a locked door, the door would still remain closed.

If anything was pursuing him and he needed to enter into the house of escape, he would not be able and he would be captured because the door was closed. If he needed to enter the door so that poverty would cease in his life, and he got

there only to find the door closed, poverty would catch up with him right there at the door.

Let us validate this point with the passage below

1 Corinthians 16:9: For a great door and effectual is opened unto me, and there are many adversaries.

The power of closed door should not be taken lightly. If someone prays against closed doors and loses his voice in the process and the door gets opened, he has struck a good and worthy bargain. Some adversaries wanted to prevent Paul from getting into those doors. There is a pastor in our church (MFM) who failed in all the examinations he ever sat for simply because he was ignorant of the art of spiritual warfare. The only examination he did not fail was the one he did not write. He failed his West African School Certificate Examination (WASCE) six consecutive times.

There was a particular year he did not take the examination and WAEC sent him the examination result that he failed. He came to the service one day and heard a message. The message he heard propelled him to pray by the time he got home. He was resolute to know what was going on because he was tired of failure. God opened his eyes. In the revelation,

he saw all his books on the table with the sixth wife of his father sitting on them. When he saw it, he was mad with anger. He took his Bible and travelled to his home town. The brother's father had died. The six wives were still staying in the same building but in different rooms. The brother's mother was in the same building with other wives.

He got home by 6:00p.m in the evening and was greeted but he did not answer any of them. His mother greeted him; he did not answer her either. His eyes were as red as coals of fire. When it was 12:00 midnight he started prayer and began to walk up and down. He started to call fire, thunder, hailstones and lightning. It was a terrible day in that house. There was nobody that went to the toilet. Everybody stayed indoors because of the high voltage of the prayers that were going on along the corridor. He continued praying till six o'clock in the morning. Then he raised up his voice and said, "Special announcement!. I am going back to Lagos now. If I fail any other examination, I shall be back here'. Do you know that the brother never failed again?

The point is that some powers had shut the door against his academic life. He then used the bulldozing power of the Holy Spirit to force the door open.

BATTLE AT THE DOOR OF BREAKTHROUGH

Outside the door of all breakthroughs, there are terrible battles. The battle outside the door is always like the scene outside the tabernacle of Moses.

In the tabernacle of Moses, what happened outside the tabernacle was terrible. Men and women would be dragging their animals to go and sacrifice them. These animals that could smell the blood of animals who had died would be struggling against entering the tabernacle to go and die there. The animals would want to run back and the owners would attempt forcing them in. It used to be quite chaotic at he door of the tabernacle.

The most terrible war Jesus fought was at the door of breakthrough. When he was coming to the world, Herod was waiting for Him. Herod kept the door closed. Likewise, enemies can close the door so that a star would not be able to come to the world. Evil powers would start dealing with the person right from the womb.

If the victim could not be arrested from the womb, the Herods would start to pursue the child. It is unfortunate that most children who get killed prematuvely are shinning stars that are shot down.

Herod confronted Jesus at birth. When He wanted to start His ministry again, the devil came up with temptations. Jesus fought and won the battle. When He was about to go to the cross at Calvary, there was a battle at the garden of Gethsemane.

When he got to the cross, the thief was there to annoy him at the cross. The devil wanted to shut that door too.

TWENTY-THREE PROPHETIC UTTERANCES AGAINST CLOSED DOORS IN YOUR LIFE.

1. The King of Glory shall visit you in the name of Jesus.
2. The King of Glory shall turn around your captivity in the name of Jesus.
3. The presence of the King of kings shall mark the beginning of glorious things in your life in the name of Jesus.
4. Instead of regret, you will become great in the name of Jesus.
5. All the habitations of humiliation and demotion shall be scattered, battered and shattered in the name of Jesus.
6. Every power that wants to swallow your destiny shall

be swallowed up by the power of God in the name of Jesus.

7. The Lord whom you serve, who is the Alpha and Omega, shall establish His favour in your life in the name of Jesus.
8. The Lord will release unto you the restoration he had packaged for you in the name of Jesus.
9. When light meets darkness, darkness gives up. Your problem shall give up in the name of Jesus.
10. The power of God shall cause every trouble to crumble in your life in the name of Jesus.
11. God Himself shall arise and attack your lack in the name of Jesus.
12. The power for breakthrough and the power of dignity shall manifest in your life in the name of Jesus.
13. The chapter of sorrow and slavery in your life shall be closed forever in the name of Jesus.
14. Whether your enemies like it or not, you shall be ushered away from the balcony of disgrace in the name of Jesus.
15. Every obstacle in your life will give way to miracles in the name of Jesus.
16. Every frustration shall become a bridge to your miracle in the name of Jesus.
17. Every enemy that is exploring more strategies to pull

you down shall be disgraced in the name of Jesus.

18. Anyone who is carrying a residential permit to stay in the valley of defeat shall be delivered now in the name of Jesus.
19. Instead of a bitter life you shall have the testimony of a better life in the name of Jesus.
20. Every habitation of cruelty fashioned against you shall become desolate in the name of Jesus.
21. Your trials shall become the gateway to your promotion in the name of Jesus.
22. The angel shall arise and write the obituary of your oppressors in the name of Jesus.
23. Using the key of the house of David, the Lord shall open your closed doors in the name of Jesus. A-M-E-N.

WHEN THE DOOR IS CLOSED

When the door is closed, the person stays outside the door of his desired haven of rest. When the door is closed, there will be unplanned happenings. When the door is closed, there will be highly uncomfortable situations.

When the door is closed, there will be frustrating experiences. Negative things will begin to lurk around. There will be exposure to hard weather conditions. The victim would have being locked out of the arena of comfort and breakthrough. When the door is closed, there will be discontinued flow of favour. When the door is closed a person faces defeats in all facets of life. When the door is closed, there would be no normal transactions because you cannot communicate with those who are inside. When the door is closed all business ventures will be paralysed and there will be freedom of enemy operation. There will be no access to desired expectations and aspirations.

When the door is closed, there will be hindrances to the attainment one's goals. When the door is closed there will be hindrances to success and promotion. Career doors will be closed; Marital doors will be closed; Financial doors will be closed; Business doors will be closed.

When a door is closed, the victim will not have access to revelations concerning the mind of God for his life. Some powers will even prevent you from knowing who you are. When a door is closed, there will always be obstacles keeping you away from your destiny. When a door is closed, the enemy will start to hinder what is supposed to be established in your life

BLASTING OPEN THE CLOSED DOORS

There are seven kinds of prayers that can force doors open.

1. The first kind of prayer that can force closed doors open is found in the book of Matthew 18:18

Matthew 18:18: Verily I say unto you, Whatsoever ye shall bind on earth shall be bound in heaven: and whatsoever ye shall loose on earth shall be loosed in heaven.

This kind of prayer is called the prayer of binding and loosing. The initiative to bind or loose comes from the earth here. The heavens get surprised and embarrassed when you ask them to work without any raw material. But, when you start to operate from the earth, angels will begin to ascend and descend for your sake. If you bind nothing here on earth, nothing will be bound for you in heaven. If you loose nothing on earth, then nothing will be loosed for you in heaven. If there is a strongman behind the door, then bind that strongman. If the enemy has shut the door, then you will open the door so that you can gain entrance inside.

There is an unwelcome development going on in the business world. Often, Christians are persecuted in their places of their work. Many times, a Christian is removed from his position and replaced with an unbeliever. Even when promotions are due, Christians are persecuted and the ungodly are promoted. Believers should see this occurrence as an attack and must rise up to save the situation. The enemy should not be allowed to continue to cheat and prey on you.

You should not see the works of the devil as "one of those things". Don't keep your legs and fingers crossed and watch your life going down the drain. Do not agree with the music of the enemy that, "What will be, will be and what goes up must come down". Take your destiny in your hands and fight your way through to victory. The Lord has given you the authority to bind and loose.

2. The second kind of prayer that opens closed doors is found in Genesis 32:24-26.

Genesis 32:24-26: And Jacob was left alone; and there wrestled a man with him until the breaking of the day. And when he saw that he prevailed not against him, he touched the hollow of his thigh; and the hollow of Jacob's thigh was out of joint, as he wrestled with him. And he said, Let me go, for the day breaketh. And he said, I will not let thee go, except thou bless me.

This kind of prayer is called wrestle prayer. Wrestling is the most aggressive of all the martial combat arts. It is quite unlike boxing with several rules to adhere to. In wrestling, anything goes. That is the reason the Bible says that we do not wrestle against flesh and blood but against powers, against principalities, against rulers of the darkness of this world and against spiritual wickedness in high places.

Wrestling in prayer means that, you allow the fire of your prayer to keep burning for a long period of time. It also means refusing to give up and refusing to be discouraged.

3. The third kind of prayer that forces closed door open is described in Isaiah 49:25

Isaiah 49:25: But thus saith the LORD, Even the captives of the mighty shall be taken away, and the prey of the terrible shall be delivered: for I will contend with him that contendeth with thee, and I will save thy children.

This is the prayer of confrontation. It is contending in prayer. This kind of payer is to bring to pass God's contention over your enemy. It is a prayer that causes God to fight on your behalf. And when God is fighting for you, be rest assured that you are a winner already.

God may be quiet for a long time. But, the day He will arise will be a terrible day for the enemy.

4. The fourth kind of prayer that forces closed doors open is found in the book of Matthew 11:12.

Matthew 11:12: And from the days of John the Baptist until now the kingdom of heaven suffereth violence, and the violent take it by force.

This is violent prayer. When you are involved in this kind of violent prayer you will pray until there are tangible result.

The prayer warrior who involves himself in this kind of violent prayer never takes a "NO" for an answer.

5. Another kind of prayer that forces closed doors open is located in the book of Isaiah 37:14-20

Isaiah 37:14-20: And Hezekiah received the letter from the hand of the messengers, and read it: and Hezekiah went up unto the house of the LORD, and spread it before the LORD. And Hezekiah prayed unto the LORD, saying, O LORD of hosts, God of Israel, that dwellest between the cherubims, thou art the God, even thou alone, of all the kingdoms of the earth: thou hast made heaven and earth. Incline thine ear, O LORD, and hear; open thine eyes, O LORD, and see: and hear all the words of Sennacherib, which hath sent to reproach the living God Of a truth, LORD, the kings of Assyria have laid waste all the nations, and their countries, And have cast their gods into the fire: for they were no gods, but the work of men's hands, wood and stone: therefore they have destroyed them. Now therefore, O LORD our God, save us from his hand, that all the kingdoms of the earth may know that thou art the LORD, even thou only.

This is a prayer called report prayer. It is the same kind of prayer that the apostles prayed in Acts 4 when they were beaten up and sent away. See the way the prayer goes in Acts 4:23-30

Acts 4:23-30: And being let go, they went to their own company, and reported all that the chief priests and elders had said unto them. And when they heard that, they lifted up their voice to God with one accord, and said, Lord, thou art God, which hast made heaven, and earth, and the sea, and all that in them is. Who by the mouth of thy servant David hast said, Why did the heathen rage, and the people imagine vain things? The kings of the earth stood up, and the rulers were gathered together against the Lord, and against his Christ. For of a truth against thy holy child Jesus, whom thou hast anointed, both Herod, and Pontius Pilate, with the Gentiles, and the people of Israel, were gathered together, For to do whatsoever thy hand and thy counsel determined before to be done. And now, Lord, behold their threatenings: and grant unto thy servants, that with all boldness they may speak thy word, By stretching forth thine hand to heal; and that signs and wonders may be done by the name of thy holy child Jesus.

It will be spiritually advantageous to report all the closed doors to God in prayer.

6. **The sixth kind of prayer that forces closed doors open is found in Job 22:27-28**

Job 22:27-28: Thou shalt make thy prayer unto him, and he shall hear thee, and thou shalt pay thy vows. Thou shalt also decree a thing, and it shall be established unto thee: and the light shall shine upon thy ways.

The sixth kind of prayer is called the prayer of decree. There is a child of God in this country Nigeria. He was doing his business quietly. The people from his home town came and said to him, "You must become our king". He said, "I don't want to be a king over you. If I should become your king it means all the idols, juju, charms and masquerades would not be allowed to operate. And I would also have a chapel in the palace. And we shall worship Jesus Christ". They said, "We agree". The brother was made king. He refused all their demonic ceremonies. A few months after he took over, the chiefs came and said, "Now that you are here, you must worship the gods of our fathers. The masquerade must come out". Then, controversy started between the king and the chiefs.

One of the chiefs happened to be very wicked. That was the chief who threatened the first king who died within 24 hours after his threat. The wicked chief said, "Okay, I will deal with you". The new king wrote a letter to us for prayer support. The king gained access to one of our books, "*Pray your Way to Breakthroughs*. The king started doing night vigils. As he finished his vigil one night, all of a sudden he found out that a monkey opened the window and got inside. He stared at the monkey and the monkey stared at him. The king then said, "Monkey, I arrest you in the name of Jesus. Remain and stand at permanent attention". The monkey then stood.

The king said, "Now I ask you a question; Are you a monkey or a human being?" The monkey refused to talk. The king went inside and took a big club and when the monkey saw the big club, it spoke in "Yoruba" dialect. The king no longer listened to the monkey. He smashed the head of the monkey and, quickly, before anybody knew what was happening, he had buried the monkey. He pretended as if nothing happened. The next morning there was a report at the palace that five chiefs were dead. You must learn how to decree through prayer.

7. The last kind of prayer that opens closed doors is called "Ephphatha" prayer. "Ephphatha" means 'be opened'. It is

a prayer that demands an opening as written in Revelation 3:7

Revelation 3:7: And to the angel of the church in Philadelphia write; These things saith he that is holy, he that is true, he that hath the key of David, he that openeth, and no man shutteth; and shutteth, and no man openeth.

The prayer of Ephphatha uses the keys of the house of David.

PRAYER POINTS

1. **My heavens open and water my ground in the name of Jesus.**

2. **Every wicked gate blocking my ways die in the name of Jesus.**

3. **Any brass over my head be shattered in the name of Jesus.**

4. **Any iron under my feet melt away in the name of Jesus.**

5. **Oh! Open heaven follow me wherever I go in the name of Jesus.**

6. **Every Joshua in me arise by fire in the name of Jesus.**

7. Every power of my father, house closing door against me die in the name of Jesus.

8. Every power of my mother's house closing door against time die in the name of Jesus.

9. Every padlock of darkness fashioned against me die in the name of Jesus.

10. You door of all-round breakthroughs open by fire in the name of Jesus.

CHAPTER THREE

TWICE DEAD

The text for this chapter Is taken from the book of Jude

Jude 12: These are spots in your feasts of charity, when they feast with you, feeding themselves without fear: clouds they are without water, carried about of winds; trees whose fruit withereth, without fruit, twice dead, plucked up by the roots.

The phrase to be noted in the passage is "Twice dead".

Let us consider another passage.

Psalm 49:16-17: Be not thou afraid when one is made rich, when the glory of his house Is Increased; For when he dieth he shall carry nothing away: his glory shall not descend after him.

The third Scripture which will give us added insight to this message is found below

Eccl. 5:15: As he came forth of his mother's womb, naked shall he return to go as he came, and shall take nothing of his labour, which he may carry away in his hand.

Another equally related reference is found in 1 Timothy.

1 Timothy 6:6-7: But godliness with contentment is great gain. For we brought nothing into this world, and it is certain we can carry nothing out.

Many years ago, there was a man on earth whom people thought was the Anti-christ. His name was Adolph Hitler. I once read a story about him which happened to be very strange to me. He caught a German spy who was spying for the enemy troop. When the German spy was brought to him, Hitler asked, "What kind of punishment should I give to this man"? He then said, "This man must die twice"! He gave instructions to his soldier, "Tie him to the stake and shoot him". He then warned the members of the firing squad that he must not die.

The man was shot at both hands but they avoided the heart and the head of the man. They got some doctors to treat him so that he would not die. The man was taken to the hospital and the bullets on his body were removed. He was fed well until he became strong again.

When he regained his health, Hitler commanded that he should be tied to the stake again and shot dead. He concluded, "The man ought to die twice".

There was a beautiful sister who came to one of our branches. She was a member of another church before she joined MFM. Her life was stagnant and nothing was progressing for her. She was a beautiful singer and a wonderful praise leader.

The great "But" in her life was that everything was stagnant for her.

She then came to the church and went for counseling. She was duly attended to. The counsellor told her two things

1. "You need deliverance"
2. "You need to leave the church where you are dancing every Sunday. You need prayers".

She agreed with the man of God and started coming for the services. She also came for deliverance. After spending two weeks in MFM, she was promoted and was given a car. She also rented a house. People started to come to her for marriage. Immediately she had all those breakthroughs, she stopped coming for the services.

She went back to her "dancing" church. One day, the white man who owned the company came to her office. The white man was the one who was instrumental to her promotion and its attendant blessings of a house and a car. The same white man met her in the office and said, "Why are you sitting on this chair and what are you doing on this table"? She said, "I am the Assistant General Manager". The white man asked, "Of which company"? The woman replied, "Of this company?". The white man asked, "Who promoted you?" She said, "You did Sir". He fumed, "No! No! No! It must be a mistake!" The man did not only demote her, he collected the car form her and the next day she was sacked. She then ran back to the MFM church.

She attended the service once after the incident. On the following day, she was found dead in a car as a result of strange bullet from the exchange of gun shots between the armed robbers and the police.

I want you to pray thus: "Every power that will take me away from my place of destiny, die in the name of Jesus".

These days are not days of backsliding. If anyone should backslide now it will spell doom for the individual. If anyone backslides the enemy would kill the person before he or she thinks of coming back to the faith. The devil will never give the opportunity for a backslider to retrace his or her steps. Anyone who falls victim to this evil agenda is twice dead.

DEATH-THE ARCH ENEMY OF MAN

Death is inescapable. It is the surest thing on earth. Everybody on earth is a dead man on leave. There is nothing on earth as inevitable as death. It is the unavoidable enemy of man. People hate death with a perfect hatred. Many even ignore death as if it will not come. Many try to defy death. Many attempt to forget about it. Some people wish for its postponement it.

Many believe that death is for some people but it is not for them. Death is the silent but ever-present enemy of man. Death is the final mystery.

Death is the ultimate deadline. It is the ultimate let or release. That is why the Bible says, "Seeketh thou anything for thyself? Seek them not" Seek the most important thing for yourself. Life is the corridor while death is the door. Death reminds us of our brief stay on earth. It is an inevitable appointment.

Jesus prayed for Lazarus to rise from the dead and it was so. But, he had to die the second time.

Death is the only last and true democracy. All men will, at last, be equal in death. There is no president, minister, governor or professor in the republic of the grave. Death reminds us of our mortality. It shows us that we are just human beings. No matter how big a person is, the moment he stops breathing for about five minutes the next thing is for him to be like the carcasses of the fowl. A time is coming when that great landlord will give you notice that your time here on earth has expired and that you need to move.

Death has been the source of many scientific experiments and studies. Yet, men do not understand death. People are afraid of death. The fear of most people is that of death. Death can do many things that no other can do. Men have studied it; men hated it, men detested it, and they have tried whether they can stop it but none has stopped it. Kings and leaders of wonderful authority were buried by death. Champions, warriors, sports men, and dictators were swept off by death.

Popular entertainers, comedians of notes, politicians and celebrities were held by death. Popular artists, notorious criminals, boxers and wrestlers who believed they were unbeatable were gotten rid of by death. Great leaders who read and wrote great books were slain by death. People who thought their money could get them everything are nowhere today. Death has taken them away. Famous and unbeatable athletes are nowhere to be found. Stars are no longer applauded again because death has swept them off the scene of life. All these people with no exception exception bowed to this great enemy called death.

The wealthy cannot buy death. The strong or mighty can not fight death. The intelligent cannot outsmart death. The legal giant in court cannot argue against it and succeed. The famous cannot entreat and impress death. The acute and astute businessmen cannot cheat death. Death accepts no deal from anybody. Death is a mighty leveller. It levels everybody. That is why no one really wants to die.

Death accepts no price and respects nobody. It was death that stopped the race of Adolph Hitler. There were many giants in this country but death dealt with all of them without exception. The Jesus of Oyingbo in Lagos, Nigeria, who proclaimed himself as the real Jesus in 1964 was terminated by death. He is no more. Many popular people have gone. Where is late Chief Awolowo? Where is late Chief Nnamidi Azikwe? Where is that Afro beat musician, Fela Anikulapo? Where is late General Abacha? Where is chief M.K.O Abiola? Where is Late I.K Dairo? Where is late Haruna Ishola? All of them are gone! Where are the former academic gurus? Gone!

Who do you really think you are? You may think you are very young and that you will always be alive. You may be wrong for in a five minutes interval, death could knock you off.

There was a particular professor who had five daughters. He was in the lecture room doing his normal teaching assignment and news got to him that his wife had just been delivered of a baby boy. He was so excited tha he jumped up for joy. Before his legs could touched the ground he was dead. Death is an inevitable appointment which everyone must keep.

It really does not matter the kind of songs that are sung at your burial. Most of the songs are fake, for no one could tell where the departed soul has gone. We were once in a christian wake and we were chased out by occult members. They came in their convoy and chased us away. Yet, before their arrival we had sung "Blessed is the death of the righteous".

THE FEAR OF DEATH

There are two reasons people fear death. People fear death because of the fear of the unknown. What is the fear of the unknown? Those of us who are born again might know that one way or the other we are satisfying or pleasing God. But unbelievers can never tell what would happen to them immediately they close their eyes in death. For those who think that they are still young and want to enjoy their lives, I recommend that they should pay a visit to the mortuary and see the dead bodies. It would amaze them that majority of those who died are the young ones.

If you do not know where you are going, you will be afraid of death. If you are not in good standing with God, you will be afraid. If you have never seen the vision of heaven you will be afraid of death. If there are sins still hiding in the laboratory of your heart, you will be afraid of death.

The second reason men fear death is because of neglect or ignorance of their destinies. The most unfortunate tragedy is that many people die for no reason.

TWICE DEAD

Any believer who goes to hell fire would be dead twice. He was physically dead before and Jesus brought him back to life and he later died spiritually.

There is one thing worse than experiencing untimely death. It is the inability to fulfill one's divine destiny. If you die without fulfilling your divine destiny, you are twice dead. A lot of people die without living fulfilled . Some even proclaim, "I possess my possession". But they have never seen such possessions before not to talk about claiming it. How will you be claiming what you have never seen? What many are calling their possessions are crumbs on the table of the enemy which they were able to pick up.

Many are living like an egg that refuses to be hatched. So, they have gone bad. When a man refuses the incubation of the Holy Ghost and is not hatched, he will decay and die.

The people I am sorry for mostly are the people who die before they are fully born. But, you do not need to die while you are in the womb of destiny. Everyone is born to complete an assignment. The Bible says that there is a time and a season for everything. Everything God created has a purpose. There is a time and a season attached to it.

You were not born into the world to be roaming about in life. God will not allow you to be conceived at all if there is no divine assignment for you. You were born for a purpose. I urge you to discover what you were born to do and do it as quickly as possible. If you die without fulfilling your purpose, then you have died twice. You have denied the present generation of your contribution. Then, you have also denied future generations of your input. Then, you will die unfulfilled. The point being stressed here is that you are born to do something and there is a time scheduled for it. Your life span is from the womb to the grave. Your time begins the minute you were born. If you do not discover what you were born to do, it means you will be wasted because time will never wait for you.

Time is an unfriendly personality. It does not wait till you find God's will. Life is mere labour until you find out why you are on earth.

If two purposeless people marry each other what will be the resultant effects? It will be like adding zero to zero. Both of them will become zero raised to the power of two. Life will be a waste of time until you find out what you have come to life to do.

Many are doing what they are not meant to do. Something says within them that they are not at their best position. These set of people have not discovered their purpose in life.

If God's will for you is to get out of this country through a visa lottery fine let it be. But, if care is not taken, the visa lottery could be a diversion of God's purpose for your life.

The enemy has given visa lottery to some people when their breakthrough was about to take place in their fatherland. They run overseas and began to suffer. I remember what happened to my father's friend. As the vice principal of a school, he had a house. Somehow, he traveled out of the country. He looked for work overseas and the only one he could secure was the job that involved washing dead bodies. He was told, "Can you do it"? He said, "Yes". When the mortuary was opened to him and he saw massive dead bodies of white people he fainted. He was rushed to the clinic and was revived. By the time he was revived, he was sacked including other Nigerians who were working there. This man was wasting away because of lack of purpose in life.

You will waste your life if you do not know why you were born. If you are almost thirty and you do not know why you are born then there is a problem. That is why at the age of thirty many people get nervous. At forty you are half way down the road. If you do not know what to do at the age of forty then you need spiritual overhauling and deliverance. If at fifty you are still roaming about, then you are finished unless you cry unto the Lord.

Death itself is a comma and not a full stop. Because after death, you will go and face somebody who will ask, "Why did you not fulfill your destiny?" It is tragic to spend three quarters of one's life without any input.

There are many confused people in the society. The women of Jerusalem were crying for Jesus. He turned to them and said, "Do not weep for me, weep for yourself and your children". Jesus implied that He had fulfilled His assignment while they were still the ones on earth.

Growing old or living long is not important to God, but finishing the assignment he has given out to His people is of paramount importance to Him. Ask yourself "What have I done with my life so far?"

For the fact that the master would one day say, "Well done" implies that the master expects you to do something. When you have not done what He expects you to do then He will tell you "I know you not".

If you know what God has sent you to do on earth, you will not have time for drinking and smoking. You will not have time for fornication. There will be no time for gossip. There will be no time for telling lies. Any lady who understands her destiny will not become a prostitute. Sinners who do not know why they are here are generally get involved in destiny-killing activities.

Death will bring into reality what you have not done. Although there is a set time for every man to live and to die, sometimes Mr. Death may cut short the time. But, if death is about to kill you, you can tell death, "Sorry, you cannot kill me I have not finished my purpose in life". If death comes, do you have something convincing to tell Mr. death?

You are born to give something substantial to the world; something which only you can give. If you die without giving it, then you are in trouble. I read of a story sometimes ago. Many soldiers were wounded and were dying at the war front. Military surgeons were brought to the war front. They were going from one body to another to check if there is anyone who was still alive. As a surgeon was moving about he heard a voice, "Here, here". It was an eighteen year old soldier who was dying. The surgeon said, "I am here I will do everything possible to help you". They boy said, "Surgeon I was not calling you". The surgeon said, "But who were you calling when you were saying, "Here, here?" The dying soldier said, "Sir about ten minutes ago, they began to make roll call in heaven I heard my name about three minutes ago and I answered those angels saying, "I am here. I wasn't calling you. You can go Sir". The soldier closed his eyes and went to be with the Lord. He had fulfilled his assignment.

You are twice dead if you do not know why you were born. You are twice dead if you do not know the reason for living. You are twice dead if you do not know the level of your personal significance. You are twice dead if you do not know God's personal plan for your life. You are twice death if you do not know heaven's record concerning you. You are twice dead if God looks at you and said, you are weighed and found wanting.

You are twice dead if you are rebellious. Rebellion is like witchcraft. You are twice dead when your life has no meaning. You were twice dead when you are contemplating taking your life. You are twice dead when your life does not count. You are twice dead when your life makes no impact on others. You are twice dead when your life is having a negative impact on others. You are twice dead when God's highest purpose for your life is frustrated.

What is God's highest purpose for your life? It is for you to be conformed to the character of Jesus Christ. Once you fail you are twice dead. You are twice dead when your life does not bring glory to God, but to the devil. You are twice dead when what you chase most are worldly desires. You are twice dead when you are sexually loose. You are twice dead when you do not know your dreams. You are twice dead when your talents and abilities die before you die. You really need to pray. Don't be caught twice dead!

PRAYER POINTS

1. Every power of darkness writing Ichabod on my destiny die in the name of Jesus.

2. Thou power of God, withdraw my steps from the wrong way in the name of Jesus.

3. Oh heavens! Come down into my dream life in the name of Jesus.

CHAPTER FOUR

THE GENERATION OF GOATS

This chapter shall be based on a peculiar parable from the book of Matthew.

Matt 25:31-34: When the Son of man shall come in his glory, and all the holy angels with him, then shall he sit upon the throne of his glory: And before him shall be gathered all nations: and he shall separate them one from another, as a shepherd divideth his sheep from the goats: And he shall set the sheep on his right hand, but the goats on the left. Then shall the King say unto them on his right hand, Come, ye blessed of my Father, inherit the kingdom prepared for you from the foundation of the world

Matt 25:41: Then shall he say also unto them on the left hand, Depart from me, ye cursed, into everlasting fire, prepared for the devil and his angels:

Matt 25:46: And these shall go away into everlasting punishment: but the righteous into life eternal.

All the people in the world fall into two categories – the sheep and the goats. These are the two categories which the human race falls into regardless of age, status, gender, tribe or nation. There is none in between the goats and the sheep. The unfortunate thing is that both the sheep and the goats could be found in the house of God. Peter cried unto the people of his

generation on the day of Pentecost that they should deliver themselves from the wicked generation.

THE DAY OF SEPARATION

The Bible warns that a day of separation would come. Right now, the sheep and the goats are doing things together. They preach together, sing together, talk together and do praise worship together. But separation will come one day. The sheep shall be separated from the goats. The sheep shall go to the right hand and the goats to the left hand. The sheep shall have eternal life but the goats shall be condemned to eternal punishment. This truth is sober and thought provoking. It can evoke tears from a preacher. Many people who are found in the church are not sheep. A day will come when they will be eternally condemned to hell.

If you have lost your parents and they died in the Lord, there is nothing to be sad about. But, if they did not die in the Lord, even if they died at old age, one should shed tears because they have gone into eternal perdition. They are gone and gone forever. They have gone with the generation of the goats.

THE RECIPIENTS OF POWER

Many are praying and crying for the power of God. Many are crying day and night that they want to be on fire for God. What most of these people do not know is that the power of God will only descend on those who are sheep.

This is a lesson we can learn from the baptism of Jesus Christ. The Scripture says that when he was baptised, the heaven opened and a voice came from above saying, "This is my beloved Son, hear ye him" The book of Matthew puts it this way.

Matt 3:16: And Jesus, when he was baptized, went up straightway out of the water: and, lo, the heavens were opened unto him, and he saw the Spirit of God descending like a dove, and lighting upon him.

The heavens were opened for Jesus and the Spirit of God descended like a dove and lighted upon him. The spirit of God came on Jesus because he was the delight of His father. He was the lamb of God and not a goat.

Men and women who pray and cry day and night should examine their lives whether they are goats or sheep. The Dove will only descend on the sheep when we cry "Let the fire fall" Be sure it will only fall on the lambs and not the goats.

When the goats start to sing "Fire fall on me!", The fire will say to the goat, "Oh goat, did you say I should fall on you?. If I fall on you then you will die" This is the secret behind the tragedy of powerlessness among present day Christians. If you are a goat, you cannot demonstrate the power of God.

Many times during deliverance, I have seen people vomit pins, lizards, tortoise, cowries, nylon bags, rags, books, living snakes, fish etc. Imagine a person with all these kinds of things in him or her beginning to say "Anointing fall on me". The anointing will stare at the person saying, "If I fall on you with all these strange objects in you trouble will come".

It is better for the goat not to call for fire because if he does he will be asking for more trouble.

GOAT KILLED A MAN!

I once read a title in a daily newspaper "Goat killed a man". The man happened to be a hunter who just came back from his hunting expedition. The man cleaned up his gun and placed it by the wall near where he had some cocoyams. Anytime the goat came, it would try to scatter the cocoyams with its leg. The man would drive it away. The goat would then move away.

After some time, the goat would be back scattering the cocoyams again. One way or the other, the goat got close to the gun and while it was scattering the cocoyams with its leg pressed the trigger of the gun. The bullet was fired and hit the hunter. That was how the hunter died. Physical and spiritual goats can be dangerous.

CHARACTERS OF GOATS

If you study the character of goats, the following facts will emerge.

1. Goats always use their head to hit anything either doors or buckets. Goats can hit other goats too with their heads. Many so called believers are like goats. They are fighters who often threaten not to greet certain people until Jesus comes.

2. Goats always eat the wrong things. Under normal circumstances they are supposed to eat wheat or grasses.

But, they would not eat those things. They might eat nice flowers which they should not eat. They might get to where there are loaves of bread and scatter them. Some strange goats eat nylon!

The enemy could make his victim to start eating rubbish. He can also feed the person with nonsense. The Lord your God has prepared food for you on the table and He is beckoning on you, "Come and dine". If you ignore the Lord's table and start to feed on insects, cockroaches, flies at the devil's table, you will develop stomach trouble.

3. Goat will not stay inside the cage. They will always want to break free. The power and strength needed to maintain five hundred sheep could be used to maintain two goats. In management, two goats are equivalent to five hundred sheep. Goats are very difficult to govern. Many church goers are like goats in this wise.

4. Goats are very stubborn. What you do not want goats to do would be their delight. Jesus was made a scapegoat so that we can be delivered from goat-like conduct . Jesus as it were was taken out into uninhabited wilderness like a

goat and was released to wander in the wilderness. He is your substitute. You have no business being a goat because Jesus was made a scapegoat for you.

5. Goats are not friendly. The Bible says something very interesting about the last day. It says that on the last days people will be unthankful; men and women will be ingrates. You might end up your life helping somebody, and because these are the last days, the person helped may turn against you. You could spend the whole of your money to send someone to school and the person may turn against you when you need assistance from him as an old man. These is one of the signs of the last days.

6. Goats are rebellious. They are highly rebellious. When you rebuke a goat, "Get away from here!" It will say, "No I will not get away". The bottom line is that the goat-like spirit is bad and destructive. If a person is likened to a goat, it means he possesses bad, destructive habits.

If you do not deal with all these bad and destructive habits, you will go to hell fire even if you go for deliverance 2,000 times. Many Christians find it difficult to break their bad habits.

You may ask, "What is an habit?" An habit is an established practice. It is an established manner, or behaviour. It is a life pattern put into practice.

Our habit affects our present life and it also affects our eternal destiny. There is need to sit and carefully see to the needs and ways of eliminating evil habits. If not, everlasting punishment shall be the portion of people with evil and bad habits. There is need to examine our lives and deal with all evil traits. A bad habit is a constant practice that is pleasing to the devil. The devil is always happy seeing it done. The bondage of habit is so light, that you can hardly feel its gravity at the beginning. Later it will develop strength and muscle in such a way that you can not cope with it.

Take for example, most of the people who are chain smokers today started in a very little mild way. They began with smoking one stick of cigarette in a month until it developed to addictive smoking on daily basis.

Sin looks simple. It is when you seek to break away from it. It is then you will realise it has great strength . By the time you start to attack sin in your life, it is then you will realize that it has

a kind of hidden and resisting power. That is why the Bible says that ye have not resisted unto the shedding of blood.

I want you to patiently go through the following Scripture and work on them

Gal 5:19-21: Now the works of the flesh are manifest, which are these; Adultery, fornication, uncleanness, lasciviousness, Idolatry, witchcraft, hatred, variance, emulations, wrath, strife, seditions, heresies, Envyings, murders, drunkenness, revellings, and such like: of the which I tell you before, as I have also told you in time past, that they which do such things shall not inherit the kingdom of God.

1 Cor 6:9-10: Know ye not that the unrighteous shall not inherit the kingdom of God? Be not deceived: neither fornicators, nor idolaters, nor adulterers, nor effeminate, nor abusers of themselves with mankind, Nor thieves, nor covetous, nor drunkards, nor revilers, nor extortioners, shall inherit the kingdom of God.

If these things are in your life as a pastor, then you are like a spiritual tout and a religious bus conductor. A pastor who is found with all these things is like a signboard pointing to a place but remains fixed to a spot.

The flesh is like a tree with different branches. In some lives the branches produce anger. In some lives the branches

produce idolatry. I ask you, "Is the goat spirit in you?"

EXAMINE YOURSELF

Are you a sheep or a goat? Sheep love one another. They do not bite one another. I ask you, "Do you have the tendency of exalting yourself?" If so, you are a goat.

Do you boast and take pride in your anointing and power when you are not even recognized in heaven? If so, you are a goat. Do you have a secret spirit of pride? You may not verbalise it but it resides in you. If so, you are a goat. Do you think that you are better than others because of your beauty, talents and academic background? If so you are a goat. Do you have an unteacheable and independent spirit that when you hear the word of God you reject it by saying. "This is not for me. That is for me?" Do you have the disposition to hate correction?

Do you have the ability to throw scathing, bitter and acidic words on people? Do you have traces of anger and impatience in you? If so you are a goat. Do you have an argumentative and talkative spirit? Do you have the disposition to criticize and find fault and you hate if you are not noticed? Do you mix the compromise spirit with your faith when no one is around? That is when nobody is around you, you change your standards?

Do you have the spirit of envy in you? Do you have unpleasant feelings about the prosperity of another person? Do you find fault with those who are more talented and appreciated than yourself? Are you dishonest? Do you cover up the truth? Do you cover up your humility? Do you exaggerate? Are you easily discouraged at the face of pressure? Do you lack concerns for lost souls? Do you lack power with God and are not satisfied with your position? Examine yourself thoroughly and then you will know if you have the spirit of a goat in you.

Are you so proud that you never greet anyone but insist that people must greet you first? Are you the type that if people are not in agreement with you then you will never greet them?

Do you take eternal issues lightly? Do you seek the approval of men for what you are doing? Are you still smoking and drinking alcohol? Are you such a person who owes people but never pays back? Are you the kind of person who always looks for people to see vision for you? Are you easily dejected and unhappy? Are you the kind of believer who is living above his spiritual experience? Are you always late to every meeting? Lateness is a bad habit. These habits are so firmly established that there is need for concerted efforts towards breaking loose from them.

Kindergarten Christianity will not survive in these last days. It will be difficult to survive. There is need to instill military discipline into your life. Allow for the discipline of the word of God in you.

WHAT YOU NEED TO DO TO BREAK THE ATTITUDE OF THE GOAT

1. Sincere Repentance: This must be done on a daily basis. Keep a short account with God. Do not allow sin to pile up. Immediately you make any mistake ask God to forgive you. Repent and never go back to your sins. If you go back to your old sins, the old sicknesses and the old demons will come back.

2. Apply the word of God to all your situations. The Bible says: "Thy word have I kept in my heart that I might not sin against you".

3. Discipline yourself: Examine what Paul said in one of the epistles.

1 Cor 9:27: But I keep under my body, and bring it into subjection: lest that by any means, when I have preached to others, I myself should be a castaway.

The human body is prone to rebellion. It does not want to take to instructions. It must be forced to obey or comply with God's order.

4. **Pray aggressively for a change in your spiritual life: One great prayer point that could be prayed is "Oh Lord, change my life by fire" The Lord is ready to change your life if you are ready to cry unto him. I want you to raise your hands and pray thus:**

   "Oh Lord change my life by fire in the name of Jesus"

5. **Avoid wrong company. Remember the word of God.**

Prov 22:24-25: Make no friendship with an angry man; and with a furious man thou shalt not go: Lest thou learn his ways, and get a snare to thy soul.

This is a very strong Scripture. If your fiance is already beating you when you are yet to get married, listen to God's instruction "Make no friendship with an angry man" The Bible

says, "Evil communication corrupts good manner" Avoid the company of goats. Bad friends will always reinforce evil things in your life. You must avoid all ungodly associations. If the best friend of a believer is an unbeliever, we can simply conclude that both of them are unbelievers.

If someone looks like a duck, walks like a duck and behaves like a duck we can conclude that the person is a duck.

6. Seek for deliverance if prayer and fasting fails you.

7. Be filled with the Holy Ghost. Once you are filled with the Holy Ghost, there is no other thing that can occupy your life.

The more you fill a cup the more the chances of getting space for other thing decreases. Once it is filled to the brim there is no space again for any other thing.

8. Do not give up: Certain people give up easily after much struggles to be freed from certain things. But we should not lose hope, we should not give up. The Bible has this to tell us

Prov 24:16: For a just man falleth seven times, and riseth up again: but the wicked shall fall into mischief.

To get rid of a bad habit may take a long time because the human flesh finds it easy to be magnetised to evil. Let God set you free from all evil habits today.

PRAYER POINTS

1. Every power of rebellion in my heart die in the name of Jesus.

2. I refuse to be a candidate of hell fire in the name of Jesus.

3. Every satanic plantation in my heart die in the name of Jesus.

4. Arrows of breakthrough fight for me in the name of Jesus.

5. Hidden darkness go out in the name of Jesus.

6. Thou stronghold of backwardness die in the name of Jesus.

Other Publications By Dr. D. K. Olukoya

1. Be Prepared
2. Breakthrough Prayers For Business Professionals
3. Brokenness
4. Born Great, But Tied Down
5. Can God Trust You?
6. Criminals In The House Of God
7. Contending For The Kingdom
8. Dealing With Local Satanic Technology
9. Dealing With Witchcraft Barbers
10. Dealing With Hidden Curses
11. Dealing With The Evil Powers Of Your Father's House
12. Dealing With Unprofitable Roots
13. Deliverance: God's Medicine Bottle
14. Deliverance By Fire
15. Deliverance From Spirit Husband And Spirit Wife
16. Deliverance Of The Conscience
17. Deliverance Of The Head
18. Destiny Clinic
19. Drawers Of Power From The Heavenlies
20. Dominion Prosperity
21. Evil Appetite
22. Facing Both Ways
23. Fasting And Prayer
24. Failure In The School Of Prayer
25. For We Wrestle ...
26. Holy Cry
27. Holy Fever

Other Publications By Dr. D. K. Olukoya

28. How To Obtain Personal Deliverance (Second Edition)
29. How To Pray When Surrounded By The Enemies
30. Idols Of The Heart
31. Is This What They Died For?
32. Limiting God
33. Meat For Champions
34. Overpowering Witchcraft
35. Personal Spiritual Check-Up
36. Power Against Coffin Spirits
37. Power Against Destiny Quenchers
38. Power Against Dream Criminals
39. Power Against Local Wickedness
40. Power Against Marine Spirits
41. Power Against Spiritual Terrorists
42. Power Must Change Hands
43. Pray Your Way To Breakthroughs (Third Edition)
44. Prayer Rain
45. Prayer Strategies For Spinsters And Bachelors
46. Prayers To Move From Minimum To Maximum
47. Prayer Warfare Against 70 Mad Spirits
48. Prayers To Destroy Diseases And Infirmities
49. Praying Against The Spirit Of The Valley
50. Praying To Dismantle Witchcraft
51. Release From Destructive Covenants
52. Revoking Evil Decrees
53. Satanic Diversion Of The Black Race

Other Publications By Dr. D. K. Olukoya

54. Silencing The Birds Of Darkness
55. Smite The Enemy And He Will Flee
56. Spiritual Warfare And The Home
57. Strategic Praying
58. Strategy Of Warfare Praying
59. Students In The School Of Fear
60. The Enemy Has Done This
61. The Evil Cry Of Your Family Idol
62. The Fire Of Revival
63. The Great Deliverance
64. The Internal Stumbling Block
65. The Lord Is A Man Of War
66. The Prayer Eagle
67. The Pursuit Of Success
68. The Seasons Of Life
69. The Star In Your Sky
70. The Secrets Of Greatness
71. The Serpentine Enemies
72. The Slow Learners
73. The Snake In The Power House
74. The Spirit Of The Crab
75. The Tongue Trap
76. The Way Of Divine Encounter
77. The Wealth Transfer Agenda
78. The Vagabond Spirit
79. Unprofitable Foundations
80. Victory Over Satanic Dreams (Second Edition)

Other Publications By Dr. D. K. Olukoya

81. Violent Prayers Against Stubborn Situations
82. War At The Edge Of Breakthroughs
83. When God Is Silent
84. Wealth Must Change Hands
85. When You Are Knocked Down
86. Woman! Thou Art Loosed.
87. Your Battle And Your Strategy
88. Your Foundation And Destiny
89. Your Mouth And Your Deliverance
90. Adura Agbayori (Yoruba Version Of The Second Edition Of Pray Your Way To Breakthroughs)
91. Awon Adura Ti Nsi Oke Nidi (Yoruba Prayer Book)
92. Pluie De Prières
93. Esprit Vagabondage
94. En Finir Avec Les Forces Maléfiques De La Maison De Ton Père
95. Que l'envoutement périsse
96. Frappez l'adversaire Et Il Fuira
97. Comment Recevoir La Délivrance Du Mari Et De La Femme De Nuit
98. Comment Se delvrer Soi-même
99. Pouvoir Centre Les Terroristes Spirituels
100. Prières De Percées Pour Les Hommes D'affaires
101. Prier Jusqu'a Remporter La Victoire
102. Prières Violentes Pour Humilier Les Probl6mes Opiniâtres

Other Publications By Dr. D. K. Olukoya

103. Le Combat Spirituel Et Le Foyer
104. Bilan Spirituel Personnel
105. Victoire Sur Les Rêves Sataniques
106. Prayers That Bring Miracles
107. Let God Answer By Fire
108. Prayers To Mount With Wings As Eagles
109. Prayers That Bring Explosive Increase
110. Prayers For Open Heavens
111. Prayer To Make You Fulfill Your Divine Destiny
112. Prayers That Make God To Answer And Fight By Firc
113. Prayers That Bring Unchallengeable Victory And Breakthrough Rainfall Bombardments

ALL OBTAINABLE AT:

1. 11, Gbeto Street, Off Iyana Church Bus Stop, Iwaya Road, Iwaya, Yaba,. P. O. Box. 12272, Ikaja, Lagos.
2. MFM International Bookshop, 13 Olasimbo, Street, Onike, Yaba, Lagos.
3. IPFY Music Connections Limited, 48, Opebi, Salvation Bus Stop (234-1-4719471, 234-0833056093)
4. All Mfm Church Branches Nationwide And Christian Bookstores.